Principles of Financial Wellness
By Bonnie Yam

Copyright @2018 by Bonnie Yam

All rights reserved. No part of this book may be reproduced or transmitted in any form or by any means, electronic or mechanical, including photocopying, recording, or by any information storage and retrieval system, without written permission from the publisher.
For information, email info@pensionmaxima.com.

Please visit our website: www.financialwellnesstower.com

First Printing: September 2018

Pension Maxima Investment Advisory
www.PensionMaxima.com

Financial Wellness Tower
www.FinancialWellnessTower.com

INTRODUCTION

Habits matter. Good habits matter. How do we nurture good financial habits? We need to understand the principles and the logical framework behind them. The Principles of Financial Wellness book covers age-old wisdom on investments and savings, and key components of retirement income planning.

Master these nuggets, build them into your day-to-day life so financial wellness becomes just a simple outcome of your day-to-day habits.

Where attention goes, energy flows.

"The journey of a thousand miles begins with one step."
–Lao Tzu

When your financial wellness improves, your confidence and opportunities will expand.

Success is on the way!

For more learning, please visit our website www.financialwellnesstower.com

About the Author

Bonnie Yam is a Chartered Financial Analyst and an Enrolled Agent with 9 financial titles to her name. She graduated from Smith College with a BA in Mathematics and Economics. She received an MBA in Finance from University of Chicago. Before starting her Qualified Plan business sixteen years ago, she was a Financial Manager for TIME Magazine, New York, and Hedge Fund Research Analyst for Cheetah Investments, Hong Kong. Bonnie has extensive experience in investment management, investment fiduciary, and investment education. She is a member of CFA Institute, NYSSCPA and FPA Association. When she isn't thinking about numbers, she likes to play piano and write jokes about the people around her.

Acknowledgements

This book is dedicated to all those who have inspired my diligent pursuit of knowledge. Success is attainable by being prepared and that is achievable only through constant learning.

This book is a compilation of my knowledge and experience in counseling 401(k) participants. I wish to thank them dearly for sharing their experiences with me. I also want to thank everyone for their insightful remarks and wonderful feedback. It has helped unleash flashes of innovation.

Finally, I want to thank my family, and special thanks to Raoul Pascual of WYNK Marketing (www.WYNKmarketing.com) who illustrated and designed this book. They have walked tirelessly by my side on this fun journey.

Thank you for your support.

Disclaimer

This book is designed to provide accurate and authoritative information on the subject of personal finance. It is sold with the understanding that neither the Author nor the Publisher is engaged in rendering legal, accounting, or other professional services by publishing this book. As each individual situation is unique, questions relevant to personal finances and specific to the individual should be addressed to an appropriate professional to ensure that the situation has been evaluated carefully and appropriately. The Author and Publisher specifically disclaim any liability for loss or risk which is incurred as a consequence, directly or indirectly, of the use and application of any of the contents of this book.

Table of Contents

1 Overall Financial Wellness

1	Invest in yourself	10
2	Compound interest	12
3	Rule of 72: Doubling	13
4	Compounding magic + saving early	14
5	Doubling: Start 10 years earlier	15
6.	Save! Save! Save!	18
9	Saving methods	19
10	Set your SMART goals	20
11	Set your budget	21
12	Tax favored investment accounts	22
13	Tax-deferred investing	23
14	Net worth: What is it?	24
14	Net worth: A measure of your true worth	25
15	Debt servicing: Debt to income ratio	25
16	Debt-to-income ratio: A measure of your total debt	26
17	Good debt vs. bad debt	27
18	What is your credit score?	28
19	Building good credit	29

2 Special Events

20	Buying a house	32
21	Buying a car	33
22	College financing basics	34
23	Choose your career carefully	35
24	Health, life, and disability insurance	36
25	Home, car, and umbrella insurance	37
26	Maximize your tax benefits	38
27	Income tax	39

Table of Contents

3 Investment

28	Risk tolerance	42
29	Risk: Asset classes diversification	43
30	Risk: Time diversification	44
31	Risk: Invest in what you know	45
32	Risk: Invest in what you can afford to lose	46
33	Risk: Managing downside risk	47
34	Risk: Upside/downside capture	48
35	Price vs. value	49
36	Growth investing	50
37	Value investing	51
38	Income generation sources	52
39	Good investment	53
40	Tax efficient investing	54
41	Annuities	55
42	Life insurance: Insurability	56
43	Life insurance: Benefits	57

4 Retirement Economics

44	Retirement	60
45	Retirement stages	61
46	Retirement income gap	62
47	Multiple sources of income	63
48	Invest in your health	64
49	Social security	65
50	Medicare	66
51	Long-term care	67
52	Reverse mortgage	68
53	Solving for retirement income gap	69
54	Understanding tax distribution	70
55	Optimal order of distribution	71
56	Property titling and transfer	72
57	Healthcare proxies, wills, and estates	74

"Money is not the only source of happiness, but it is a great relief to know you are managing it properly."
—Bonnie Yam

1
Overall Financial Wellness

1 Invest in Yourself: Go to School

Fact: Statistics show that there is a $1,000,000 difference in lifetime earnings between High School grads vs. College grads.

1 Million Dollars

Earning Potential of a
High School Graduate

Earning Potential of a
College Graduate

Trust me. You can afford it.

*You can lose your money,
but no one can steal your education.*

Whatever your major, it will be helpful to take a course or two in Accounting, Finance and/or Taxes.

2 Compound Interest
It's the Eighth Wonder of the World!

7% return every year, 10 years = 197%
$(1.07)^{10}$ or   1.07 x 1.07 x 1.07 ... ten times = 1.97 or 197%

10% return each year, 10 years = 259%

15% return each year, 10 years = 405%

"He who understands it, earns it.
He who doesn't, pays it." —Albert Einstein

3 Rule of 72: Doubling

How long does it take to double your money?

Formula:

$$\frac{72}{\text{Interest Rate}} = \text{Number of years to double}$$

$$6\overline{)72} = 12$$

Rule of 72: Take 72, divide it by the return, and you will get the number of years it takes to double your investment.

Example:
7.2% interest ➡ doubles in 10 years
10% interest ➡ doubles in 7.2 years

It is important to start early. Each additional double becomes more significant as you start to accumulate more assets.

4 Compounding Magic + Saving Early

Scenario 1: Start early
Penny started saving at age 25. She saved $10,000 each year for **10 consecutive years**. Her total out of pocket contribution is

$100,000.
At age 65 the value is an amazing

$1,125,365.

Scenario 2: Start late
In the second scenario, Max started saving at age 35, 10 years later than Penny. Like Penny, Max saved $10,000 each year but he saved for **30 consecutive years**. However, his total out of pocket contribution is a whopping

$300,000.
At age 65 the value is only

$1,070,000.

Penny: *Hey Max, you should have started 10 years ago. You **paid more** but I still **made more!***

Compare Compounding Worksheet at 7% interest Rate

Scenario 1: If You Start at 25

Year	Beg Bal	New Contributions	Interest	End Bal
Age 35	$128,164	$10,000	$9,672	$147,836
Age 45	$271,790	$0	$19,025	$290,816
Age 55	$534,653	$0	$37,426	$572,079
Age 65	$1,051,743	$0	$73,622	$1,125,365

Scenario 2: If You Start at 35

Year	Beg Bal	New Contributions	Interest	End Bal
Age 35	$0	$0	$0	$0
Age 45	$128,164	$10,000	$9,672	$147,836
Age 55	$399,955	$10,000	$28,697	$438,652
Age 65	$934,608	$10,000	$66,123	$1,010,730

5 Doubling: Start 10 Years Earlier

Want more money?
Just start 10 years earlier!

Assuming you get a 7.2% return every 10 years, you will double your money every 10 years.

It pays to Start Early. The last compounding (10 years) is worth: $1,000,000.

Penny @ Age 70
$2,000,000

Penny: Maybe you should have started 10 years earlier.

Penny @ Age 60
$1,000,000

Max: What? You're making double of everything I make?!?

Penny @ Age 50
$500,000

Max @ Age 50
$250,000

Max @ Age 60
$500,000

Max @ Age 70
$1,000,000

6 Generate Income

Work Smarter! Get more education!

Work Harder! Part-time jobs for more pay.

... no stealing or borrowing!

7 Know Your Needs vs. Your Wants

Penny: Look what I got you for Christmas! You will probably never need them but, they were all on sale anyway.

The more I make, the more I can spend!

A Smaller Bank Statement

Max: Look what I got you for Christmas! This didn't cost a lot but, I think you will like it.

The more I make, the more I can save!

A Bigger Bank Statement

WEALTH
It is about how much you SAVE, not how much you MAKE!

8 Save! Save! Save!
More in. Less out!

"A penny saved is a penny earned."
—Benjamin Franklin

"A fool thinks every sale is always a good reason to spend."
—Raoul Pascual

There's no excuse... everyone can SAVE! Start small.

Consistent saving transforms quickly into REAL WEALTH.

9 Saving Methods
There are 3 approaches to saving.

Target Savings AFTER Expenses
Raise Income or Cut Expense to hit Targeted Savings.

 minus  equals

Earn Big! — Spend Big — Saving Goal

 minus  equals

Earn Little — Spend Little — Saving Goal

Target Savings BEFORE Expenses
Target Savings first and spend what's left over.

 minus  equals

Whatever you Earn — Savings Goal — Left over for Expenses

10 Set Your S.M.A.R.T. Goals

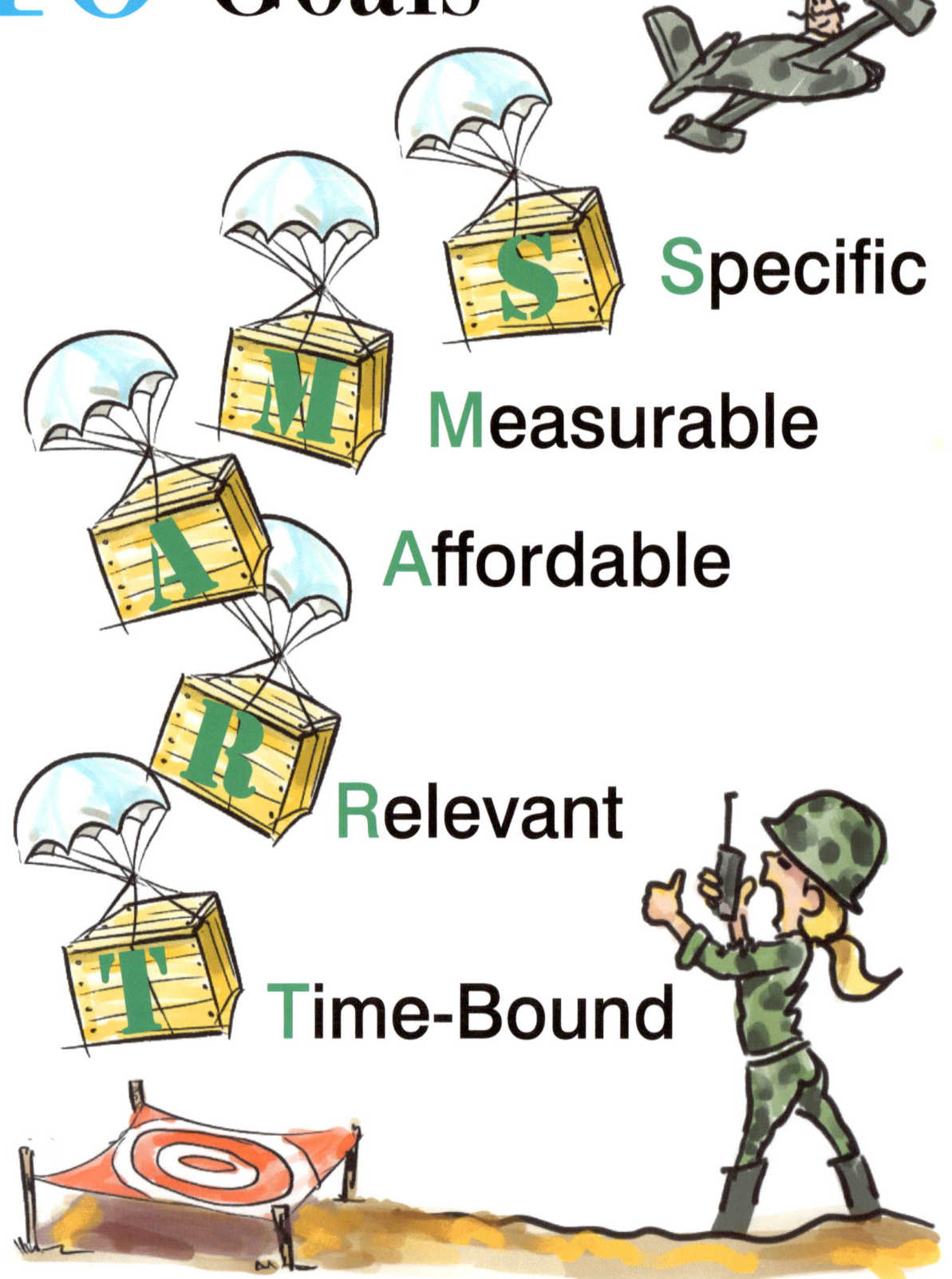

Specific

Measurable

Affordable

Relevant

Time-Bound

Not every goal is a S.M.A.R.T. goal.

11 Set Your Budget
Know Your Income, Your Expenses and What to Prioritize

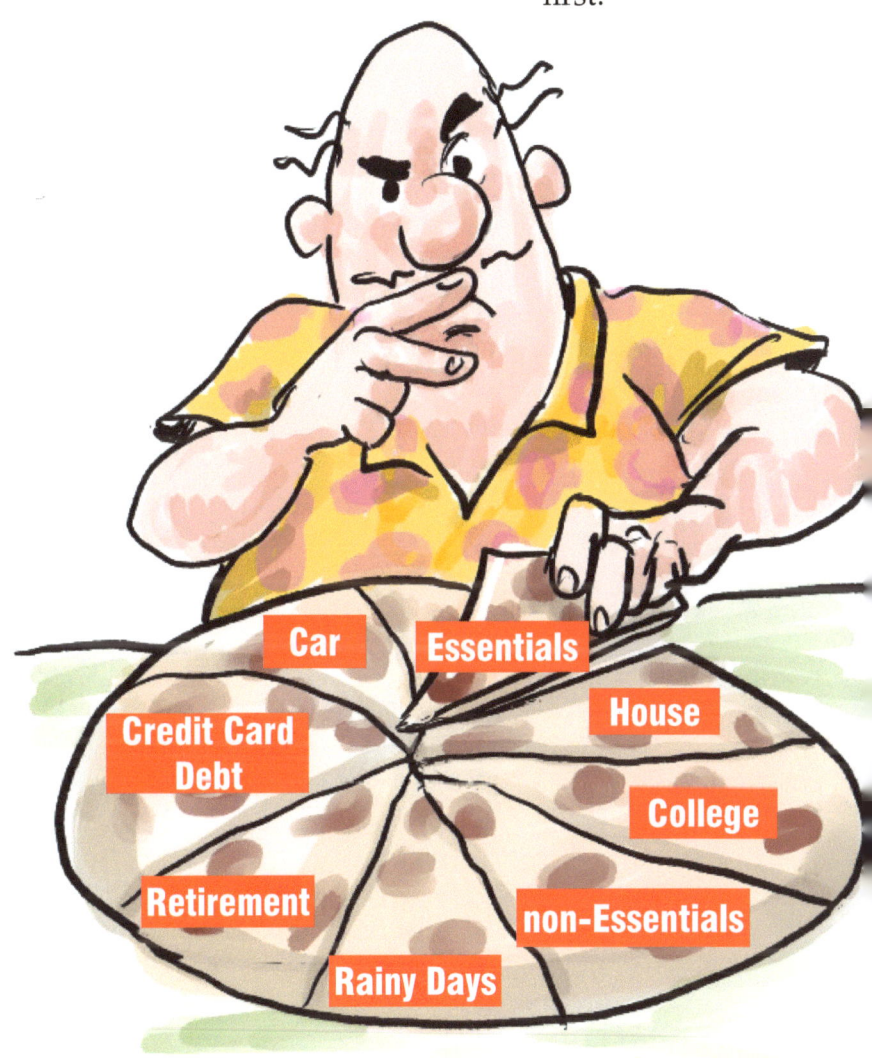

Hmmm ... I think I'll take on the Essentials first.

Expense Priorities:

1. **Essential Expense**
   What you absolutely need!

2. **Emergency Cash**
   Good for 3 months.

3. **Goals**
   Short-term: Repay debt (especially if you have a high interest rate)
   Medium-term: Down Payment for House, Car, Saving for College
   Long-term: Saving for Retirement

4. **Nonessential Expense**
   What is nice to have!

Start Early and remember to use the Magic of Compounding!

Try this if your budget doesn't balance:
- *Lower your expense* (more immediate)
- *Increase your income* (less immediate)

12 Tax Favored Investment Accounts

How to keep more of your earnings by paying less taxes

Income (What You Earn) — (Minus) **Essential Living Expense** (What You Owe)
- Emergency Cash
- Pay off Debt
- Savings Goal

(Equals) = **Cash Flow** (What You Can Spend)

Put as much as you can towards tax-favored investment vehicles.

Tax-Favored Vehicles
- Company 401(k)
- Additional IRA (income limits apply)
- Defined Benefit Plan (if you are a small business owner)
- Cash Value Life Insurance (Growth is not taxable)
- Annuities (Growth is not taxable)

I need to be smarter with my money.

Delay tax payment by investing into Tax-Favored Investment Accounts.

13 Tax-Deferred Investing

Retirement Options:

Income Tax Deferral, Tax Fee Growth:
- Traditional 401(k)
- Traditional IRA
- SEP
- SIMPLE IRA

Tax Later!

Tax Free Growth, Tax Free Distribution
- Roth 401(k)
- Roth IRA

Tax Now!

Tips:

Maximize your tax deferral by contributing to the maximum tax limits allowed by tax-favored investment vehicles or whatever is allowed by your cashflow budget. At the minimum, try to contribute enough to maximize your company match (FREE money)!

Systematic Investment Benefits:

Splitting investments into multiple payroll contributions throughout the year helps diversification. Automatic payroll deposits makes saving simple and easy.
Set it to auto-pilot!

FUTURE

PRESENT

Maximize 401(k) account contributions. At the minimum, max up to company match.

14 Net Worth: What is it?

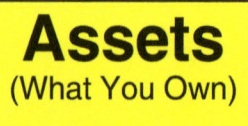  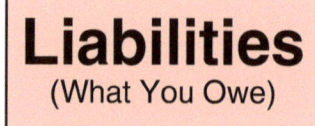 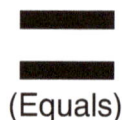

Assets (What You Own) — (Minus) **Liabilities** (What You Owe) = (Equals) **Net Worth** (What You're Worth)

US Household Net Worth Ranking in Dollar Equivalent Breakpoints	
Net Worth Percentile	**Net Worth Breakpoint**
10%	-$963
20%	$4,798
30%	$18,754
40%	$49,132
50%	$97,226
60%	$169,551
70%	$279,594
80%	$499,264
90%	$1,182,390
95%	$2,377,985
99th Percentile (Top 1%)	**$10,374,030**

15 Net Worth: A Measure of Your True Worth

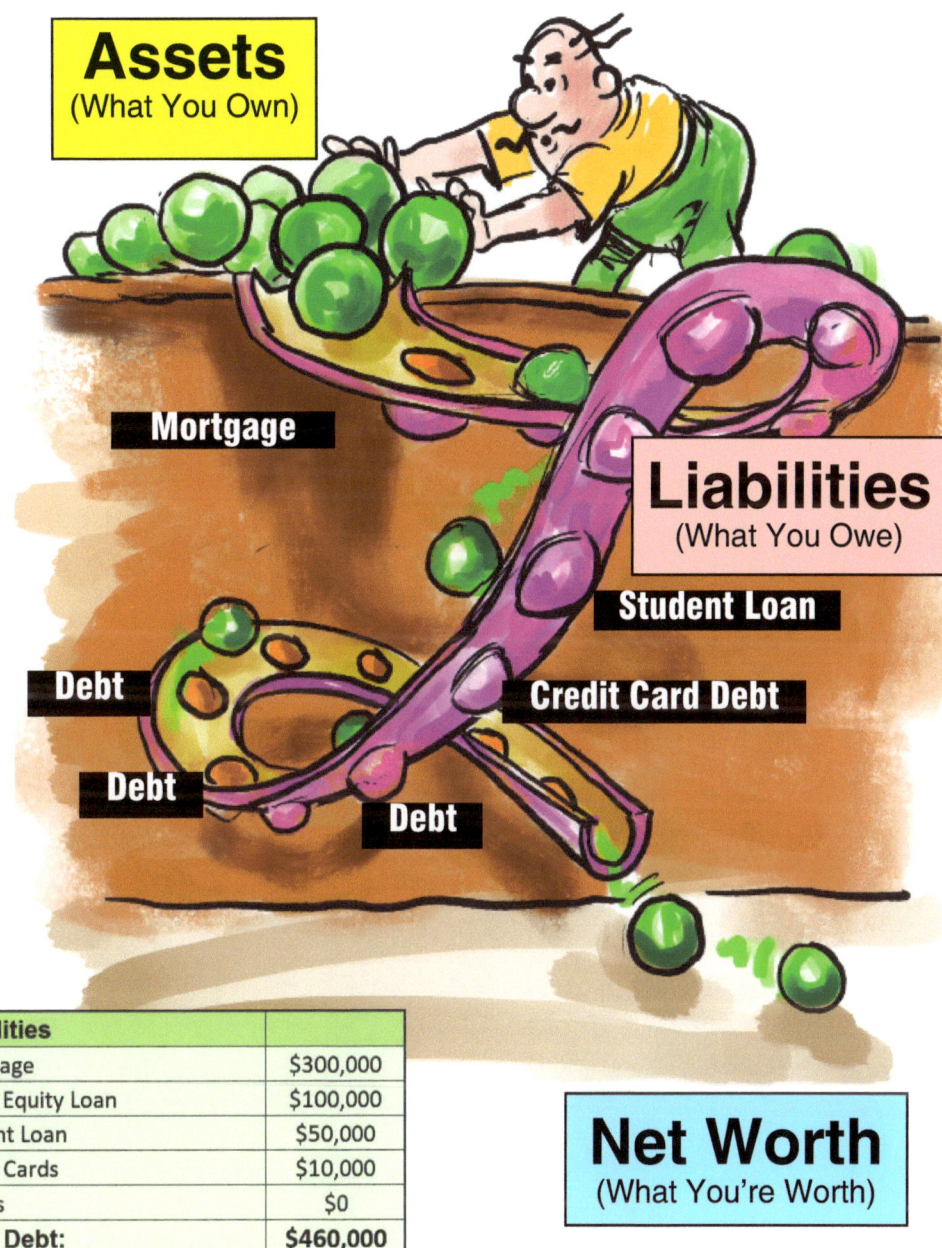

Common Assets
- Stocks
- Bonds
- Cash
- Retirement Accounts
- Primary Residence
- Vacation Home
- Art/Furnishings/Jewelry

Typical Liabilities
- Mortgage
- Home Equity Loan
- Student Loan
- Credit Cards

Assets		Liabilities	
Stocks	$100,000	Mortgage	$300,000
Bonds	$50,000	Home Equity Loan	$100,000
Cash	$10,000	Student Loan	$50,000
Retirement Accounts	$200,000	Credit Cards	$10,000
Primary Residence	$500,000	Others	$0
Vacation Home	$10,000	Total Debt:	$460,000
Art/ Furnishings/jewelery	$50,000		
Other	$0	What is my Net Worth?	
Total Assets:	**$920,000**	*Calculate:*	$460,000

Did you improve over last year? Don't measure your self-worth exclusively by your Net Worth!

16 Debt-to-Income Ratio: A Measure of Your Total Debt Burden

DTI Formula: = Total Debt Payment / Total Income

Example:
Income = $100,000   Debt Payment = $20,000
Debt-to-Income Ratio or DTI = 20%

What is your DTI* safety zone?
- **More than 20% Debt** - Danger Zone
- **15% - 20% Debt** - Caution Zone
- **Less than 15% Debt** - Safe Zone

* Debt-to-Income Ratio (Excluding Mortgage Payments)

"The borrower is servant to the lender."
—The Bible: Proverbs 22: 7

Dangerous Water Level
Cautious Water Level
Favorable Water Level

Debt

15% Debt | 15-20% Debt | over 20% Debt

DTI should be under 45% (*Including Mortgage).
Don't drown in your DTI.

17 Good Debt vs. Bad Debt

Remember: Lenders make a profit whether it's good or bad for you.

Good Debt = Investment
Examples:

- House
- Business
- Education

Good Debt Increases Long Term CASH FLOW

Bad Debt = Consumption
Examples:

- Credit card debt
- Luxury items
- Non-essentials

Bad Debt Lowers Long Term CASH FLOW

**Good debt is investment for growth.
Bad debt is just borrowing for consumption!**

18 What is Your Credit Score?

Find out from: Equifax, Experian or TransUnion www.AnnualCreditReport.com. You are allowed one free report a year.

Of course I can give you a loan. The chances of you paying me back with interest is very good.

Why is it Important?
- It affects your borrowing rate.
- Your employer, your insurer, your rental owner ask for it

Check your FICO® Score. Check for Inaccuracy of Data, Fraud, and Identity Theft. Fix and Negotiate reprieve for missed payments.

FICO® Score Calculations	
35%	Payment History
30%	Debt Level
15%	Debt Account HIstory
10%	New Debt
10%	Type of Debt

FICO® SCORE is a score to indicate your financial habits. Form Good Financial Habits. Your Credit is GOLD.

19 Building Good Credit

FICO® Scores are the credit scores used by 90% of top lenders to determine your credit risk.

If you have a good credit score, you will have lower interest expenses.

Scenario of 2 people with different FICO® scores

Good FICO® score
FICO® score: 780 => Good credit
Lending rate = 3%
3% interest on $100,000 is $3,000

Bad FICO® score
FICO® score: 580 => Bad credit
Lending rate = 6%
6% interest on $100,000 is $6,000

Difference in interest expense: $3,000

Penny: My FICO® is 780. I pay on time and establish good credit with merchants!

Max: My FICO® is 580. I can't even get a proper credit card!

Good credit gets you lower financing cost.

"Impulse buying is purchasing an item today for $20 and selling it for $1 in a yard sale tomorrow."
—Raoul Pascual

2
Special Events

20 Buying a House

It's one of the best investments to make:

- Mortage and Real Estate Taxes are income tax deductible.
- Tax Free Gains on Sale of Primary House:
    - $250,000 tax free (Single)
    - $500,000 (Married Filing Joint)
- Leverage play on Down Payment Deposit

Example:
House price: $100,000
Down Deposit: $20,000 or 20%

Historically, home values go up. So let's say your house price goes up to $120,000

New Value:	**$120,000**
minus	
Original Value	**($100,000)**
your	————
Net gain will be	**$20,000**

Wow!

Primary Home: First $250,000 is Tax FREE!

Formula:
Profit $= \dfrac{\text{Gain}}{\text{Deposit}} = \dfrac{20{,}000}{20{,}000} =$ **100%**

Buying a house builds equity, provides tax deductibility, and is also a leveraged play on return.

21 Buying a Car

Finally, you have the freedom to go anywhere... but there are costs.

New vs. Old, Buying vs. Leasing

New Vehicle	Old Vehicle
Lower rate on financing	Lower purchase price
Full warranty for 1st 36 months	Limited warranty
Latest safety features and technology	Lower registration and licensing fees
Hassle-free maintenance	More maintenance issues

Buying (financing)	Leasing
You finance entire cost of car	You finance the depreciation of lease
Higher down deposit	Lower down deposit
Higher monthly payments (life of car)	Lower monthly payments (lease term)
More expensive short-term	More expensive long-term
Cheaper long-term	Cheaper short-term
You own the car	No equity built after lease term

Don't forget: You will also need current car insurance.

Leasing requires less Cash Flow, but buying is cheaper long-term because you own the car.

22 College Financing Basics

Education = Good Debt = Investment

Rule of thumb:
Keep your college debt to no more than one time your annual salary when you graduate!

- Only borrow what you need.
- Know your interest rate, term, fees, monthly payment after you graduate.
- Max out subsidized loans first.
- Exhaust Federal Loans before Private Loans.
- You should not borrow if your tuition fee is more than you expect to earn in the first year after you graduate. If your salary will be $35k why pay for education that costs $50K? How will you pay that off?
- Keep your debt payment to under 10% of your salary, so you can finish repaying your debt in 10 years.

Lots of Debt **Minimal Debt**

Pssst! It doesn't make sense to get a student loan if your yearly tuition is more than double what you will realistically earn. Find out how much people earn in your profession. Is there a demand or a glut in your career choice?

Only borrow what you can afford.

23 Choose Your Career Carefully

A diploma helps, but it is not a guarantee.

Did you know?

2017's average college debt balance:
$39,400

2017's average college grad salary:
$49,785

When deciding what course to take, make sure you balance your abilities, the demand for the skills that you will gain, and your potential salary. Remember there are thousands of unemployed college grads with huge debts.

24 Health, Life and Disability Insurance

If you die, why would you need money?

You probably won't, but your family, your business, or your favorite charity might.

Insurance payouts can help fulfill unanticipated family needs during emergencies.

- To pay off your mortgage
- To pay off estate taxes
- Provide continued care to family members
- Smooth out transition of business

Insurance / Beneficiary / Accident Catastrophe / Death

Consider a health savings account if appropriate.

25 Home, Car and Umbrella Insurance

Why buy insurance?

To protect the stuff you own. Insurance also provides liability coverage in case you're legally responsible for accidents that cause injuries or property damage to another person.

Which insurance should you get?

- Home insurance isn't legally required by most States but it may be required by your lenders.
- Don't just get the state minimum auto insurance. Consider also an umbrella insurance to cover your assets and income.

Don't just get the minimum. Get enough to protect your assets.

26 Maximize Your Tax Benefits

Maximize your Tax Benefits through Tax Favored Investment Vehicles and Income Tax Deductibility on certain expenses.

For Investments, aim for:
- Tax deductibility against income
- Tax deferred growth
- Tax free withdrawal

Taxes

Tax Deductibles

Tax Favored Investments
- **Traditional 401(k)*:** Tax Deductible, Tax deferred growth
- **Roth**:** Tax Deferred growth, Tax free withdrawal
- Contribute to max deferral limits (if cashflow allows)
- Contribute at the minimum to maximize company match (FREE Money)!

Tax Deductible Expenses—Cafeteria Plan
- Accident and health benefits (but not Archer medical savings accounts or long-term care insurance)
- Adoption assistance
- Dependent care assistance
- Group-term life insurance coverage
- **Health savings accounts (HSA)***, including distributions to pay long-term care services

---

*   **Traditional 401(k):** Taxed at distribution (ordinary income tax)—Tax Later!
**   **Roth 401(k):** Taxed at contribution, no tax at withdrawal—Tax Now!
*** **Health Savings Account (HSA):** Contributions are tax deductible, growth is tax deferred, and withdrawal, tax free—Triple Tax Free!

Maximize Tax Deductible Investments such as 401(k) and shelter eligible expenses under the Cafeteria Plan.

27 Income Tax

Taxes that you MUST pay: Federal, State*, City*, Social Security 6.2%, Medicare 1.45%

Depending on where you live, you might not have any!

How to Calculate Your Taxes

- **Regular Income**
  (-) Deductions (1)
  Maximize here!
  = Adjusted Gross Income
    (-) Standard or
  Itemized Deductions (2) =>
  Maximize here!

Tax Deductions (1)
- 401(k)
- Cafeteria Plan*

Standard Deductions or Itemized Deductions (2)
- Medical Expenses (7.5% AGI)
- State, Local, Real Estate Tax ($10,000)
- Mortgage ($750,000)
- Charity (60% of AGI)
- Casualty & Theft
- Unreimbursed Job Expenses (2% AGI)

- **Taxable Income**
  Apply Regular Tax Rates (Check for AMT)

- **Required Tax**
  + Other Tax Due
    (-) Tax Withheld or Prepaid
  (-) Tax Credits (3)=>
  Maximize here!

Popular Tax Credit Items (3)
- Additional Child Tax Credit
- Earned Income Credit
- American Opportunity Credit

= **Tax Due or Tax Refund**

Cafeteria Plan Benefits
- Accidental and health benefits
- Adoption Assistance
- Dependent Care Assistance
- Group Term Life Insurance
- Health Savings Account (HSA)
- Education Assistance
- Employee Discounts
- Employee Stock Options

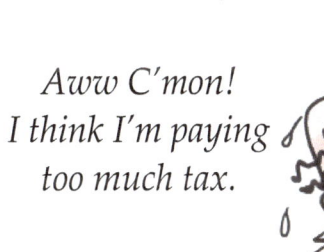

Aww C'mon! I think I'm paying too much tax.

Taxes are due on Apr. 15, with a six month extension until Oct. 15. If you can't file on time, at least pay on time! Interest on back taxes starts accumulating from Apr. 15!

"I am always doing that which I cannot do, in order that I may learn how to do it."
—Pablo Picasso

3
Investment

28 Risk Tolerance

Many factors will determine your risk tolerance

Risk Considerations:
1. Your investment time horizon. At what age do you need the money? _____
2. Your investment goals
How much money do you need to accumulate? _____
(Aggressive, Balanced, Moderate, and Conservative)
3. Your attitude towards risks (Choose).
   ☐ I can't lose
   ☐ I'm OK with losing a little
   ☐ Risk doesn't bother me
4. Your risk/return tradeoff
5. Your personal situation
   ☐ I am an experienced/novice investor
   ☐ I am really tight with money?

In midlife, you try to take moderate risks especially if you have already accumulated a nice sum of retirement money.
If you get hit badly by another financial crisis, you might have to delay your retirement.

The younger you are, the more risk you can afford.
You have more time to recover and you can earn more money.

Seniors normally have limited ability to bring in new income.
Capital preservation is important. You can't afford to lose!

The younger you are, the greater your capacity to take risks. When you get close to retirement, capital preservation becomes more important.

29 Risk: Asset Class Diversification

Asset Classes
Fixed Income [BOND]
Duration
  Short-term | Medium-term | Long-term
Credit
  AAA | AA | BBB | BB
  Government | Corporate | International

Equity:
Large | Mid | Small [STOCK]
Growth | Value | Blend
US | International | Emerging Market

Sector:
Health | Utilities | Real Estate | Commodities

What to get:
1. Conduct a risk assessment to determine your ideal portfolio given your risk appetite and anticipated investment horizon.
2. Select a stock and bond allocation that points you to the desired risk return requirement.
3. Select an allocation from different asset classes that will reduce fluctuation while aiming at the desired return.

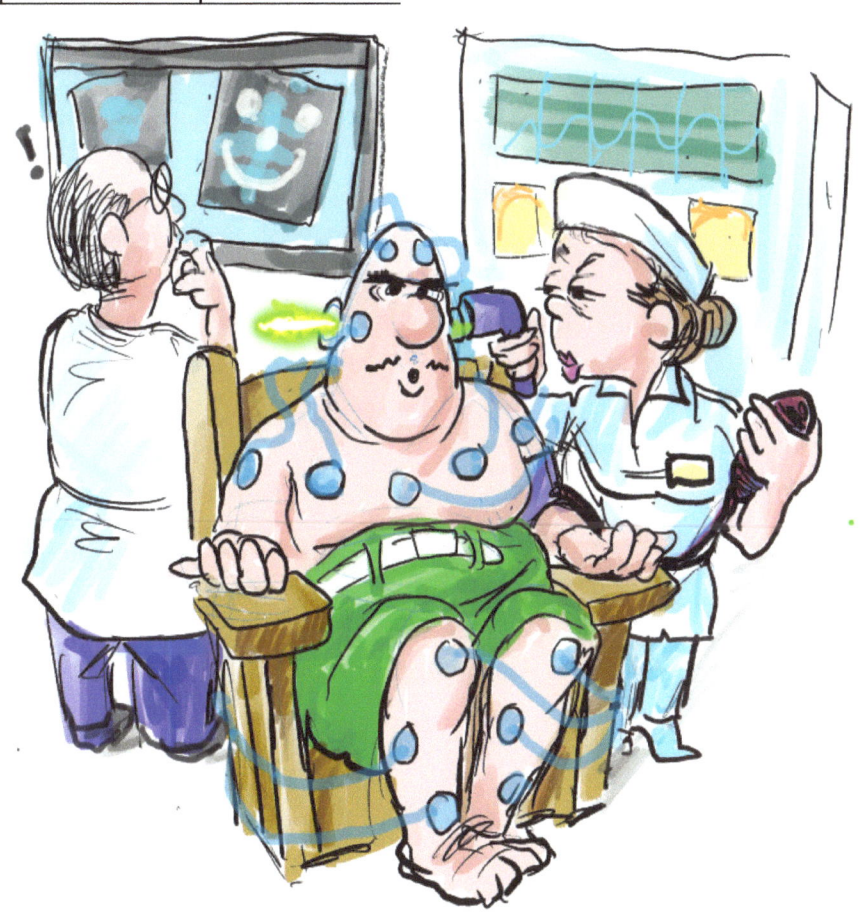

A financial planner can help assess your risk tolerance.

30 Risk: Time Diversification

Remember the crash of 2008? It only took 4 years to recover.

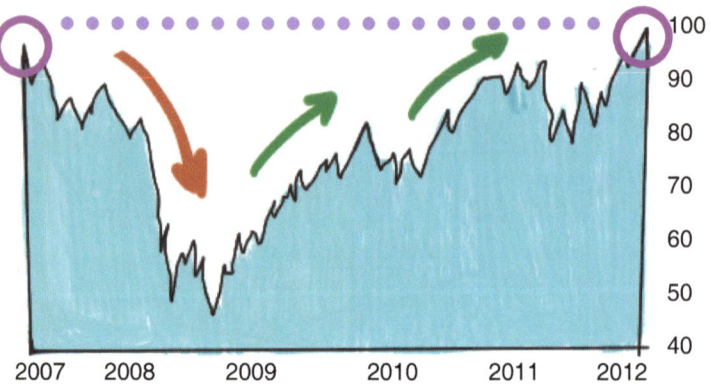

Penny: *I choose to stay invested.*
Max: *I'm worried!*
Penny: *C'mon Max! Think Big Picture!*

Time is your friend. Stay invested to counter short-term volatility. Don't let your emotions control you.

Over time, the US Stock return goes up nicely. Even if the market goes down, if you can wait, it will go back up. The longer you wait, the more likely it is that you will not lose money.
THINK LONG TERM!

31 Risk: Invest in What You Know

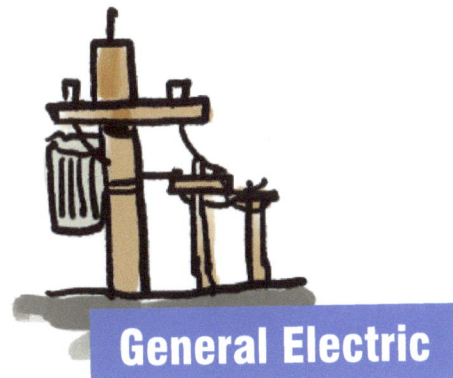

General Electric

ATT

Microsoft

Do your research well before you invest. If the fundamentals haven't changed, why worry about the market?

Q: Invest in Bitcoin?
A: Sorry, I don't know much about it.

Q: Starbucks?
A: I think I know something about it.

Q: Microsoft?
A: I think it will still be around.

Q: Am I a conservative investor?
A: Not really.

Q: Am I scared to take risks?
A: Definitely, Not!
But I only invest in what I know.

Starbucks

Home Depot

"Rule No. 1: Never lose money.
Rule No. 2: Don't forget rule No. 1."
—Warren Buffet

Know what you own. Don't take excessive risks.

32 Risk: Invest in What You Can Afford to Lose

If you are not willing to own a stock for 10 years, do not even think about owning it for 10 minutes.

"In the short run, the market is a voting machine, but in the long run it is a weighing machine."
—Benjamin Graham

Max: The Dow Jones Industrial Index dropped 800 points?!?! That's OK.
I still like what I bought.

Enjoy the ride without being over-worried.

33 Risk: Managing Downside Risk

Why is it important to have a limit on how much you should risk? When you lose money, your capital shrinks. With a lower base, you need a much higher return to get back to where you were before.

It is much harder to gain money after losing it.

34 Risk: Upside/Downside Capture

Good Upside Capture: When you win, you want to win more than the average market.

Good Downside Capture: When you lose you want to lose less than the average market.

Good Upside Capture and **Decent** Downside Capture

Low Upside Capture and **Poor** Downside Capture

Objective of Downside Capture: Don't lose too much.

UPSIDE CAPTURE measures the upside performance relative to the market.

DOWNSIDE CAPTURE measures the potential loss relative to the market.

UPSIDE CAPTURE
- >100 above average upside capture in up markets
- <100 below average upside capture in up markets
- 100 means market equivalent upside capture in up markets

DOWNSIDE CAPTURE
- >100 above average downside capture during down markets
- <100 below average downside capture during down markets
- 100 means market equivalent downside capture during down markets

Look for a higher upside capture ratio and a lower downside capture ratio.

35 Price vs. Value

How do you price real value?
Low Price, Good Product = GOOD VALUE

1. **Pricing Tricks**
   If yesterday it was $10 a pair and today it is $20, but 50% off, it's still $10 a pair!

   No REAL VALUE

2. **Good News Expectation**
   Future Amazon Headquarter
   New Apple Product

   GOOD VALUE From Anticipated Growth

3. **Relative Pricing (volume based)**
   Costco
   Retail supermarket pricing advantage due to order volume

   Better relative pricing in industry

4. **Temporary Market Distortion**
   Temporary Samonella incident

   Good Companies when everyone is selling GOOD TEMPORARY VALUE

5. **It's expensive, but it's worth it!**

   Good Product, Reasonable Price – RIGHT VALUE

The Trap

REALITY CHECK: Cheaper parts, Low quality labor, Second hand used car.

TRUST ME! This baby uses all brand new parts!

Be able to distinguish what is real value.
Is it Pricing Tricks, strong Relative Pricing in Industry, temporary Price Distortion, value from Anticipated Growth Prospect, or Real Value?

36 Growth Investing

A growth stock is a stock that is anticipated to grow at a rate significantly above the average of the market. These stocks tend to trade higher relative to its fundamentals.

More downside — Market Drop

Anticipated Growth

Fair Market Value = $100

Current Market Value = $120 — What you are paying today

100% Growth Expected Market Value = $200

INVESTMENT STRATEGY:
Price Increasing because of great Growth Prospects

Growth Examples:
- Amazon
- Facebook
- Google

WATCH OUT!
Don't just follow the crowd by buying what what seems to be growing fast. Stocks may be overpriced already.

Growth Variables to look for
- Earnings Growth
- Sales Growth
- Cash Flow Growth
- Book Value Growth
- Long Term Projected Earnings Growth

***Growth* without *Value* offers no *Investment Merit*.**

37 Value Investing

A value stock is a stock that tends to trade at a lower price relative to its fundamentals, making them more appealing to value investors.

Less Downside
Market Drop

Anticipated Return

Current Market
Value = $70

Fair Market
Value = $100
What you are paying today

10% Growth Expected Market
Value = $110

INVESTMENT STRATEGY:
Price Increasing to catch up to Fair Market Value

Value Examples:
- Verizon
- Royal Dutch Shell
- Wells Fargo

WATCH OUT!
The stock value may be too good to be true. There may not be any more room to expand.

Value Variables to look for
- Price to Book
- Price to Sales
- Price to Cashflow
- Dividend Yield
- Price to Projected Earnings

Hmmm... is that what I hope it is?

Value without Growth offers Limited Upside.

38 Income Generation Sources
Where to raise cash

1. **Fixed Distribution (at retirement):**
   - Pension
   - Annuities
   - Social Security Income
   - Required Minimum Distribution from 401(k)

2. **Income from Gov't and Banks**
   - Bank CDs
   - Government Bonds (depending on term)
   - Municipal Bonds (watch for credit rating)

3. **Dividend from Blue Chip Stock***

   Share of large well-established and financially secure company

4. **Income from Corporate Entities**
   - Domestic Corporate Bonds
   - Foreign Bonds

   Safety depends on: TERM, CREDIT, COUNTRY

5. **Real Estate Rental Income**
   - Watch out for bad tenants, vacancies

6. **Cash from Liquidating Current Investment Portfolio**

7. **Income from Part-Time Job**

8. **More Unconventional:**
   - Limited Partnership
   - Oil and Gas
   - Reverse Mortgage

Aim for multiple sources of income. Rank them by liquidity, safety, and return. Match safe returns to essential expenses. Be prepared to delay expenses if returns don't match up.

39 Good Investment Metrics
How do I pick Investments?

Look out for:

- **Good top line growth:**
  Sales, Revenue growth
- **Good bottom line growth:**
  Net Income growth compared to similar industries and all other industries
- **Good Debt Control:**
  Debt/Equity Ratio < 0.5?
- **Good Cashflow:**
  Positive and growing?
- How long has it been in business?
- Is the stock selling at a discount to fair value?
- Is it a commodity product? Any competitive advantage?

- **Top line growth vs. Bottom Line growth:**
  Top line growth does not always imply healthy bottom line. There could be additional expense required to bring in the additional revenue. On the other hand, good bottom line does not always imply good top line growth. It could be a result of short term cost cutting.
- **Economic Moat:** Ability to maintain competitive advantages over its competitors in order to protect its long-term profits and market share from competing firms.

Learn by DOING! Make an Investment List and start tracking performance.

40 Tax-Efficient Investing

Understand what's Taxable, Tax-Deferred, and Tax-Exempt.

Taxable Account	Tax Treatment
Principal	After Tax Contribution
Interest	Ordinary Income Tax
Qualified Dividend	Capital Gains Tax
Gains from Sale < 1 year	Ordinary Income Tax
Gains from Sale >= 1 year	Capital Gains Tax

Difference between Ordinary Income Tax and Capital Gains Tax

The maximum federal tax rate on ordinary income is 39.6%, compared to only 20% on long-term realized capital gains; but short-term capital gains are taxed at the same higher rate as ordinary income. For higher income individuals, it makes a huge difference in how they are being taxed.

Tax advantages at different stages

Account	Contribution	Earnings & Growth	Withdrawal
401(k)/SEP/Simple IRA/Traditional IRA	Tax-Deductible	Tax-Deferred	Ordinary Income
Health Savings Account (HSA)	Tax-Deductible	Tax-Deferred	Tax-Free
Roth IRA/Roth 401(k)	After-Tax	Tax-Deferred	Tax-Free
Education 529/Education IRA	After-Tax	Tax-Deferred	Tax-Free

- **Tax Deductible:** What you contribute will not be counted as taxable income.
- **Tax Deferred:** Gains need to be reported but not taxed if the money is invested in a retirement account.
- **After Tax:** Contributions are considered taxable income and will be taxed.
- **Tax Free:** No tax assessed at distribution.

41 Annuities

Turn investment into steady stream of income at retirement.
- Fixed Annuity: guaranteed payout
- Variable Annuity: payout stream determined by investment performance
- Immediate Annuity: immediate payout
- Deferred Annuity: future payout

Advantages:
- Tax Deferred Compounding
- Guaranteed Rates of Return (Fixed Annuity)
- Guaranteed Lifetime Payment option

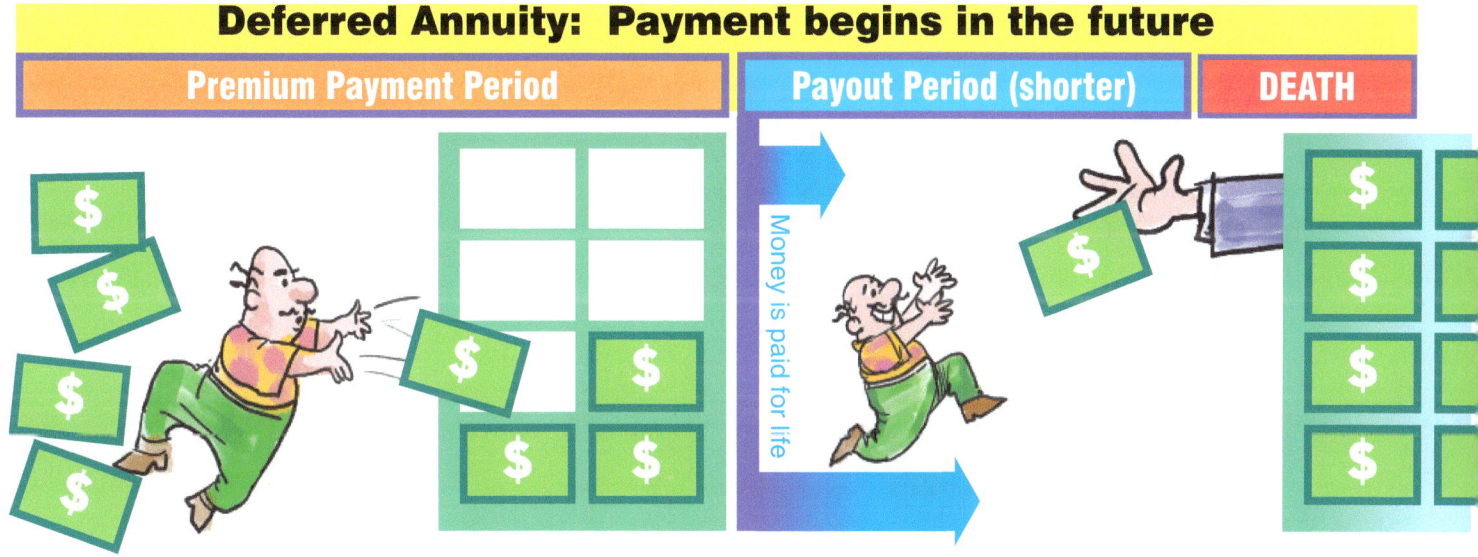

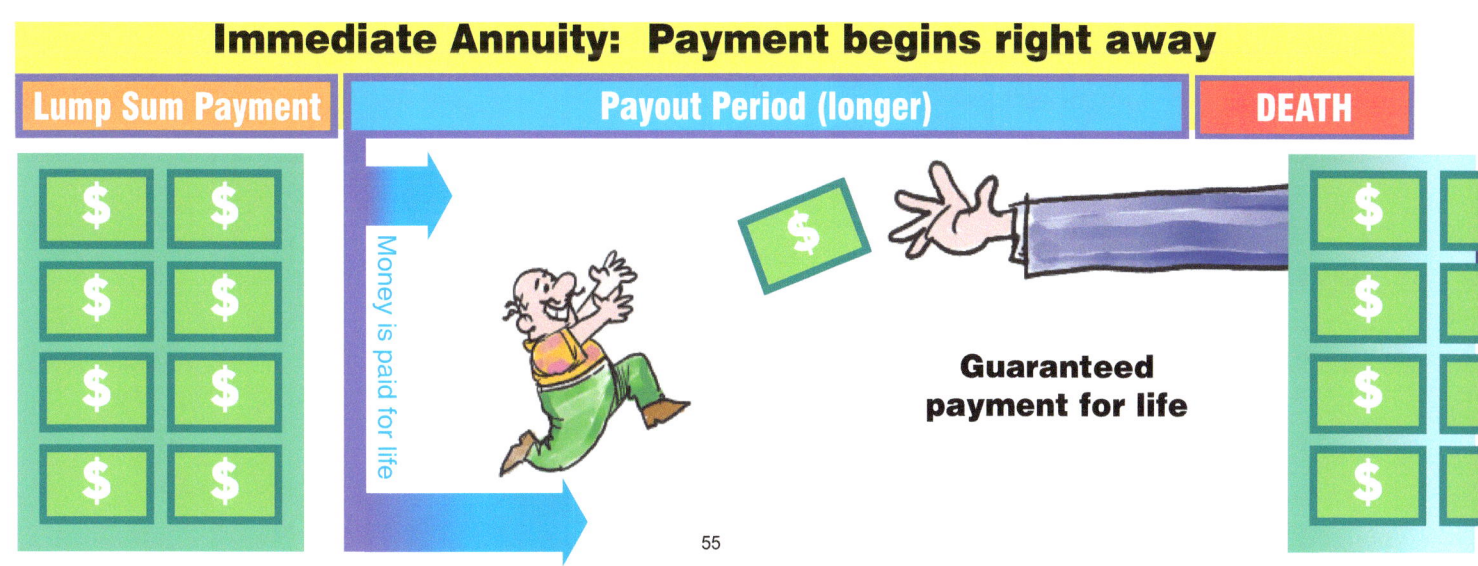

42 Life Insurance: Insurability

Factors Affecting Life Insurance Cost
1. Your health
2. Your age
3. Whether you smoke
4. Your regular activities
5. Your genetics
6. Where you live
7. The amount of your coverage
8. The duration of policy

Max: Marry me! I will buy $1,000,000 in life insurance, and you will be my beneficiary!

Penny: That's sweet, but are you even insurable?

Healthy, Non-Smoker Low Premium

Insurance Company: Let's charge him a lot! He is a high-risk client!

Overweight, Smoker High Premium

Watch out for Insurability.
The earlier you buy it, the cheaper it is.

43 Life Insurance: Benefits

TERM LIFE INSURANCE

Finite term, Cheaper
No Savings Component

Best Suited for:
- **Temporary insurance** needed to pay for end of life expenses
- Limited cashflow to fund for insurance

- Tax Free Distribution at Death
- No Cash Value for Borrowing

PERMANENT LIFE INSURANCE
(Whole Life, Variable Life, Universal Life)

Permanent, More Expensive
Savings Component or Cash Value

Best Suited for:
- **Permanent insurance** to fund for end of life expenses
- Extra cash component for tax deferred savings

- Tax Free Distribution at Death
- Cash Value for Borrowing (College)
- Riders*: Early Distribution for Medical Needs
    * additional coverage

Max: If I'm still alive by the time the sand runs out, I lose the bet!

Penny: I don't have to worry about dying anytime but boy! --- my monthly premium is really expensive!

Benefits
- Pay for Funeral and Burial costs
- Pay for Probate and Estate
- Pay for Personal Debt and Mortgage
- Pay for Medical Expense not covered by Health Insurance
- Create an inheritance for your heirs

Life Insurance provides liquidity and peace of mind when you most need it.

"I retired early for health reasons. My company was sick of me and I was sick of them."
—Anonymous

4
Retirement

44 Retirement

Stop working for a living and enjoy working at living.

Retirement is doing what you want, when you want.

Penny:
I like singing and dancing.

Max:
Me tooooo!

Retire from work, but don't retire from life.
Create new goals for the next stage of life.

45 Retirement Stages

Good News: We're living longer!
Bad News: You may suffer longer!

1. Go-Go Years:
The period immediately after retirement. Capable of more travel and hobbies. Expenses can be go higher than pre-retirement.

2. Slow-Go Years:
Health concerns start settling in. There are less activities and more stay-home time. Expenses drop.

3. No-Go Years:
Health concerns are getting serious. Spending goes up again because of expensive end-of-life care.

Spending requirements for different stages of retirement are different. Be prepared for end of life health expenses. For example, Long Term Care can be extremely expensive if you purchase it when you need it. In fact, no insurance company will want to insure you at that point.

Plan wisely for different periods of retirement. Asset spend-down is not easy, and mistakes are irreversible.

46 Retirement Income Gap

"The question isn't at what age I want to retire, it's at what income."
–Mark Twain

Retirement is not just an ending. It is also a beginning.

Determine your lifestyle and figure out your needs. Do you have enough? Should you work more? Have you covered your essential needs?

47 Multiple Sources of Income

What kind of income do you have at Retirement? Social Security? Pension? 401(k)? Investments? Annuity Income?

Annuity Income: A form of investment that translates account value into fixed income guaranteed for life.

Plan your retirement with your partner well.

Penny: I know. You still want to be a part-time teacher, but I want to travel.

Best security is to have multiple sources of income, and continue to generate part-time income.

48 Invest in Your Health

Doc: Where does it hurt?

Max: Everywhere!

Doc: My prescription for you: Exercise 20 minutes a day. Cut out fat and excess carbohydrates. Drink water, and SLEEP MORE!!

**Better health = Better Quality of Life.
"Well-thy" is Wealthy.**

49 Social Security

When should you start claiming Social Security?

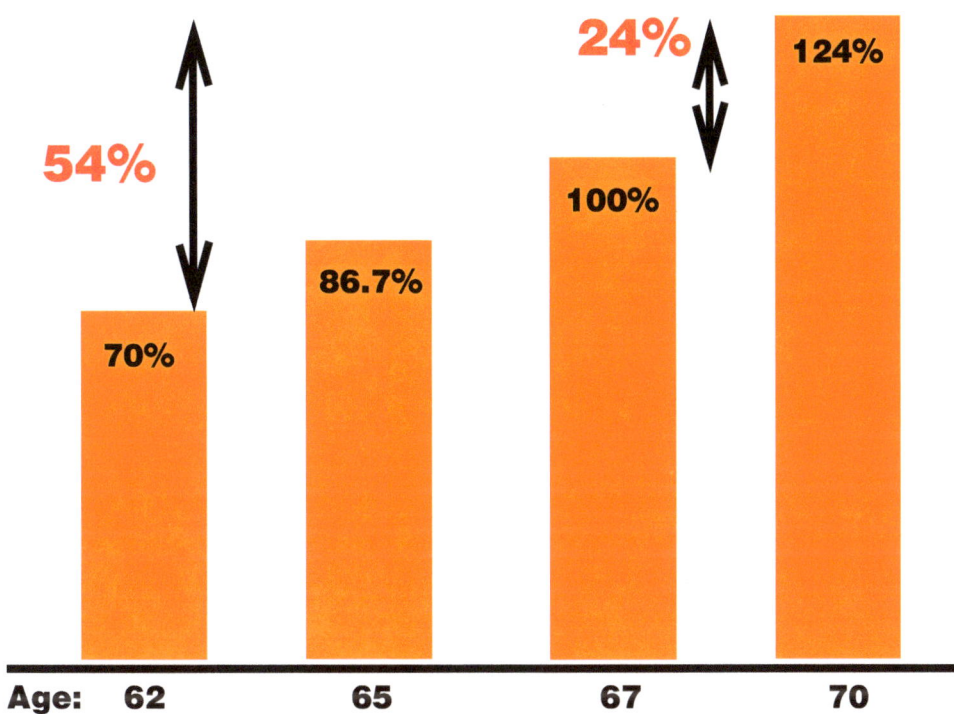

Process:
1. Determine your Normal Retirement Age or NRA.
2. Determine % reduction of income if you claim early. Claiming early at age 62 could reduce your income (up to 30%).
3. Determine % increase of income if you delay your claim. Delaying claim to Age 70 will increase income by 24%.

Total difference: 54%

So that thing really works, huh?

If you need the money, you might need early distribution. But if you are healthy and have the financial resources, it pays to delay Social Security Claims.

50 Medicare

Medicare in a nutshell: It is a government Medical Program for age 65 and up.

Part A: Hospital Coverage
Inpatient care in hospitals, including critical access and long-term care (available only if medically required)

Original Medicare:
Part A & Part B
Medicare Advantage:
Part C

Part B: Medical Coverage
Doctors' services and outpatient care when medically necessary

Part C: Medicare Advantage
Includes Parts A, B, D and Medigap

Part D: Prescription Drug
Available in stand-alone plans or as part of Medicare Advantage

Medicare versus Medicaid

Medicare only pays for medically required procedures, but not long term care. **Medicaid** funds for long term care expenses, but has strict income requirements. Any gift(s) or asset(s) transfered to lower income must be made at least 5 years prior to application in order to avoid penalties.

Yeah, I know it's complicated. Use this to start the conversation.

Comments on Costs:
Part A: FREE for most if you have Social Security coverage.
Part B: Premiums are income adjusted.
Part C: Additional premium after Part B.
Part D: Premiums are income adjusted.

What to watch out for:
1. Watch for enrollment entry period.
2. **Make sure your have creditable coverage to avoid penalty fees for late enrollment.**
3. Do you need Original Medicare or Medicare Advantage? (Depends on whether you are happy with in-network providers. Consult your Medicare Plan Finder).
4. Do you need Part D Drug Plan Cost?
5. **Do you need Medigap policies to cover deductibles and copay amounts?**

51 Long-Term Care
It is expensive. Will you be prepared?

LTC is the care you need when you can no longer perform daily tasks such as:
transferring + continence + dressing + toileting + bathing + eating

- **Self-funding**
- **Life insurance with LTC Rider**
- **Long-Term Care Insurance**
  Wealthy Clients: Age 57, assets of $200,000 excluding primary residence
- **Medicaid**
  ◊ Eligibility set by individual state
  ◊ Either Income Cap State or Spend-down State
  ◊ Spend-down State (ex. New York)
    Must Spend-down income on care until you hit State limit in order to qualify
  ◊ Income Cap State (ex. New Jersey)
    Must give away excess income to qualified trust, "Miller Trust"
  ◊ 5 year look back policy
  ◊ Any gifts or transfers of assets must be made at least 5 years from date of application to avoid penalties
  ◊ Medicaid funds for 50% of all long term care expenses

Statistically, end of life care lasts 2.2 years for men and 3.7 years for women.

Start planning early. Seek qualified advisors.

52 Reverse Mortgage
Borrow from the equity of your house to pay for living expenses

No PAYMENTS until the house is sold!! And if my house's value doesn't meet up to the loan, no worries!

There's NO TAX! It's a LOAN.

I just feel comfortable living it out in my own house, with my old neighbors

Requirements:
- Must be the primary house
- Borrower must be age 62 or older
- Must own house with low mortgage
- Must still pay for home costs like insurance and property taxes
- Must get advice from an approved HECM (Home Equity Conversion Mortgage) Counsellor before applying

Reverse Mortgage Application:
- Live in your own house while you age
- When you "**go**" your house "**goes**" to the lender

Reverse Mortgage: Good for someone whose mortgage is mostly paid off, needs cash, but doesn't want to sell. Could be EXPENSIVE! The house not available for the kids.

53 Solving for Retirement Income Gap

Do you have enough money to retire?

Retirement Income Calculator
You just failed your Target Retirement Savings exam. 2x Income = > Need 10x income. You don't have enough to retire yet!

Rule of thumb:
Target retirement savings = 10x Pre-retirement Income
Example:
At 67 (normal retirement age), salary = $50K
Target retirement savings = $50k x10 = $500K

Look up an online Retirement Income Calculator and input the following items:
- Your current age
- Your current savings balance
- Saving contributions: 401(k)/Outside *(Increase contributions if you are young, compounding effect)*
- Social Security amount *(Delay to increase benefits)*
- Withdrawal age *(Delay retirement to increase saving and delay spending)*
- At what age you want your savings to last? *(Longevity issues)*
- Your estimated expenditure at retirement *(Be mindful of health issues and different stages of retirement)*
- Other income at retirement *(Any part-time income increases cash flow)*
- Asset allocation *(More aggressive to aim for higher returns particularly if you are young)*

Strategy for the YOUNG:
- Save More Now
- More Aggressive Investment Allocations

Strategy for the OLD:
- Delay retirement
- Delay Social Security Claim
- Increase Income (Part-time job)
- Cut Expenses
- More Aggressive Investment allocations *(Be ready to delay expenses during bad performance time)*

Did you pass the Retirement Income Gap scenario? Don't worry. Redo and recast if there is a shortfall.

54 Understanding Tax Distribution

Understanding Tax Bites:
Penalties for Late or Early Withdrawals

- RMD (Required Minimum Distribution): 50% penalty if not taken at age 70 ½
  (Reason: The gov't wants you to start taking out your tax deferred savings so they can start taxing you)

- 10% Penalty on early Distribution before age 59 ½ on pre-tax 401(k)s

Taxable Items:
Ordinary Income:

- Distribution from 401(k), Annuity
- Social Security Income: Up to 85% taxable depending on Income
- Short Term Capital Gains (< 1 year)

Capital Gains Tax:

- Long term Capital gains (> = 1 year)

Not Taxable: Roth 401(k)
Roth IRA, Insurance payouts

- Could be subject to Estate Tax

Know the rules. Knowledge is POWER!

Determine which accounts to take distributions from to minimize tax consequences.

55 Optimal Order of Distribution
Know what to sacrifice first!

Order of Distribution:
- Taxable, Annuities, tax-deferred, Roth or Tax exempt
- Arbitrage. When tax rate is low, you make selective withdrawals from tax deferral accounts like 401(k) to minimize tax bite.

Goal:
- Minimize tax bite by delaying distribution from tax-favored accounts to continue to benefit from tax-deferred growth.
- If there is an external event that puts you at a lower tax rate, take distribution from the tax-favored account to pay tax at the lower tax rate.

Sustain Tax-Deferred growth by minimizing withdrawal from Tax-Favored Accounts

56 Property Titling and Transfer

Proper titling can assist in asset transfer, avoid probate, and minimize estate taxes

I own half of what you own!

I owe half of what you owe!

1. Common Law vs. Community Law Property State (Married Couples):

Common Law Property States: Ownership separate. Dependent on titling.

Community Property States: All property earned or acquired after marriage is co-owned 50/50 by the couple.

2. Tenancy

Tenants in Common: If one co-tenant dies, interest is passed to the beneficiary named in his or her will.

Joint Tenant with rights of Survivorship: If one tenant dies, the property will pass to the surviving joint tenant.

> **Probate:** It is the legal process for distributing your property after you die. Most people want to avoid probate because it can be slow, costly and it is public. You can avoid probate by establishing a living trust.

> **Pour-over will:** It ensures any of an estate's assets not already captured in a trust transfer into the trust when an individual dies.

Does it matter? Yes, if you want privacy, control, speedy distribution, and to minimize estate taxes.

3. Transfer through Probate (PUBLIC):

With a will:
Control distribution of your property. Can be used to designate a legal guardian and an executor for the estate. Need to go through a court process to verify inventory. Can be expensive and time consuming.

Without a will (Die Intestate):
Court appoints administrator to distribute property in accordance with the state laws. More Expensive.

4. Transfer through Trusts (PRIVATE):

REVOCABLE TRUST (Reversible):
Transfer assets to beneficiaries when you die. Avoid Probate. Need a Pour-Over Will to cover assets that have not been transferred. Assets not protected from creditors. Grantor pays income tax on income earned by estate.

IRREVOCABLE TRUST (Irreversible):
Cannot be dissolved or changed once created. Best used to transfer out assets with high future appreciation. Gift Tax due on transfer.

5. Transfer by Contract:
Insurance
Annuities, 401(k)
Beneficiary designation forms

Thanks for nothing Dad! All your wealth went to Uncle Sam!

57 Healthcare Proxies, Wills and Estates

Penny:
I'm so glad I prepared! I established my healthcare proxies, prepared my will and trusts...

Max:
What a mess! They put me on life support for 2 years and spent all my money.

Healthcare Proxies: A document with which a patient appoints an agent to legally make healthcare decisions on behalf of the patient when he or she is incapable of making such decisions.

Living Will: A document that explains whether or not you want to be kept on life support when you become terminally ill and will die shortly without life support or fall into a persistent vegetative state.

I am worse! I didn't know that all of a sudden, I have so many illegitimate kids.

It's about control...control while you are living and control after death.